I Ching

Text and illustrations by
CHAO-HSIU CHEN

REDFeather

MIND | BODY | SPIRIT

An Imprint of Schiffer Publishing

"Red Feather Mind Body Spirit" logo is a registered trademark of Schiffer Publishing, Ltd.
Published by Red Feather Mind, Body, Spirit
An imprint of Schiffer Publishing, Ltd.
4880 Lower Valley Road
Atglen, PA 19310
Phone: (610) 593-1777; Fax: (610) 593-2002
E-mail: Info@schifferbooks.com
Web: www.redfeatherpub.com

Originally published in 2004 as a set of cards entitled
I-Ching Cards

ISBN: 978-0-7643-5714-5

Printed in China

THE TEMPLE AND
THE I CHING

There was no wind; it was calm everywhere. The river ran gently without hurry, forming one curve after the other until it reached the ocean.

The reed beds along the shore were shaken by a group of egrets; a crowd of gulls invaded the territory, creating another breeze. One flew up suddenly from the surface of the water, with a freshly caught fish in its beak. The other birds gathered around him, creating a further disturbance.

I was following the spectacle played out by the birds before me, and my sight rose higher and higher, until it reached a golden twinkling ... It was the top of the temple tower, which seemed to glow more than I remembered. I had met the abbot there a while ago, and he had helped me to learn the way to great compassion.

I walked along the sandy riverbank, and climbed the hill to the temple. Nothing seemed to have changed. It was late afternoon, before evening prayers, and I found the master meditating in the octagonal pavilion in the garden. I put my palms together in front of my chest, and made a low bow.

"Which way has led you here this time?" the master asked me with a gentle smile.

"The way of the water," I answered respectfully, and stole a glimpse at him. His silver beard was even longer than before. He broke out laughing.

"If you have found the way of the water, which goes everywhere, even to the lowest places, then you are ready for the I Ching. I will show you the secret of it."

And so the time went by. Each time I visited the master in the temple, I learned more of the different versions of the I Ching, and I discovered an old version with the interpretations of Lai Zhi De, who was born in the fourth year of the Jia Jing reign of the Emperor Shi Zong in the Ming Dynasty (the year 1525 in the Western calendar). This version combines the different Chinese philosophies of Taoism, Buddhism, Confucianism, Legalism, and the idealist philosophy of the Confucian school in the Song and Ming dynasties, together with the deep understanding of the law of nature and changes of life.

I present this I Ching to you, based on the studies of Lai Zhi De. During my work, the voice of the master often appeared with the words:

Life comes, because it comes.
Life goes, because it goes.
Everything changed, because it happened.
Nothing remained, because it changed ...

CHAO-HSIU CHEN

5

WHAT IS THE I CHING?

The I Ching has been consulted in China for almost 4,000 years, and is considered not only an oracle to forecast the future, but also the source of all Chinese wisdom. And after Confucius's interpretation, its philosophical value was truly established.

The Chinese, in particular, are continually fascinated by the ups and downs of life in our many-faceted world. Everyone strives toward luck and good fortune, and tries to avoid anything inauspicious. Over time, the vagaries of life have shown us how governments and powerful people can fail; how dynasties can rise up and then vanish; how scholars receive both honors and humiliation; and how the poor become rich, and poor again …

Why is life so full of changes? Why is luck never permanent? How can we avoid harmful influences? These questions about our own fortunes and the nature of the universe concern us all, and each culture has its own oracles that it consults about these questions. But none is as well preserved or as effective as the oldest of them all: the I Ching.

The essence of the I Ching, or "Book of Changes," is also changing ("I" – "change," and "Ching" – "classic holy book"). Over 4,000 years ago it was this principle that led Fu Xi, the first Emperor of China according to Chinese mythology, to formulate his system of eight "trigrams." The trigrams each comprise three lines, either broken (– – Yin) or unbroken (—— Yang), and their names represent the eight universal principles or natural laws (*see opposite*). These lie at the heart of every situation, and they are based on the eight directions of heaven.

Later on, during the Shang Dynasty (1766–1122 BCE), the Emperor Zhou Wen Wang further developed Fu Xi's eight trigrams into the sixty-four hexagrams, each comprising six lines (two trigrams – an lower one and an upper one). These hexagrams make up the I Ching.

FU XI'S EIGHT TRIGRAMS

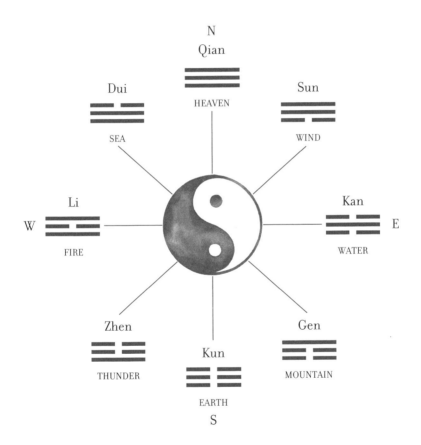

CONSULTING THE
I CHING

Traditionally, the I Ching is consulted by throwing yarrow stalks or coins, and then building a hexagram line by line. Follow the instructions below to discover how to use your coins to create a hexagram, and whether a second hexagram (formed by "moving lines") also applies to your reading. You will need a pen and paper to record each line as you go.

- Close your eyes and clear your mind, releasing sorrow and anger. Concentrate on your question, and make sure that you ask only one question at a time. The I Ching will offer better guidance if your question is clear and short. Avoid asking questions when you already know the answer, and avoid repeating questions just because you may not like the answer you receive. Remember to remain focused on your question or issue throughout the casting process.

- Now take all three coins and begin creating your hexagram. Each line is formed by throwing the three coins together and seeing whether they fall as "heads" (the side with four characters) or "tails" (the side with two characters). There are four possible coin combinations, each of which is transcribed as a particular line (*see overleaf*). Starting with

IF YOU THROW	DRAW THIS LINE
3 tails	━━×━━
2 tails, 1 head	━━ ━━
2 heads, 1 tail	━━━━━
3 heads	━━○━━

the bottom line and working upwards, throw the coins six times and record each line, until you have completed your hexagram.

- Turn to the table of hexagrams on pages 14–15: check down the left-hand side to find the lower trigram (bottom three lines) and across the top of the table to find the upper trigram (top three lines). This gives you your hexagram number. Turn to this hexagram in the book to receive insight on your enquiry.

Moving lines

If any of your lines were formed by throwing either three heads or three tails, these are known as "moving lines" (signified by either an X or an O) and indicate that a change is about to occur in the situation. These lines turn into their opposite (so, a broken line becomes an unbroken line, and vice versa), giving you a second hexagram – sometimes known as your "future hexagram" – to shed further light on your enquiry.

Each hexagram features an illustration reflecting my impression of the oracle's meaning, along with my calligraphy for the original name plus my personal interpretation of the essence of the hexagram's meaning. The first part of the text gives you a direct answer to your question, the second part offers guidance for your path, and the final part shows you how to advance, and take appropriate action.

TABLE OF HEXAGRAMS

Upper Trigram		Qian	Zhen	Kan
Lower Trigram				
Qian		1	34	5
Zhen		25	51	3
Kan		6	40	29
Gen		33	62	39
Kun		12	16	8
Sun		44	32	48
Li		13	55	63
Dui		10	54	60

Gen	Kun	Sun	Li	Dui
26	11	9	14	43
27	24	42	21	17
4	7	59	64	47
52	15	53	56	31
23	2	20	35	45
18	46	57	50	28
22	36	37	30	49
41	19	61	38	58

HEAVEN

Celebrate the sun, the earth, health, and
the beginning of the universe.

The dragon is hiding. His great personality has not yet emerged. Cultivate your own moral character, and wait for the right moment in which to act.

Strive constantly to improve yourself, and you will be able to fly high toward the sky, or to retreat into your own heart. But even if you are free from doubts, do not fly too high; no one can hold an over-filled bowl without spilling the contents.

EARTH

Follow the earth's example, to be
virtuous and humble.

The earth is soft, but it is also strong. It nurtures myriad creatures. It obeys the laws of heaven, while complying with nature. It can tolerate everything, while treating everything fairly and with kindness.

When you ask for something, do it the correct way, and with the right attitude. Uphold justice, but act gently; only through obeying the way of the earth will you attain your goal.

GERMINATION

*With the help of others you can
continue on your way.*

The seed germinates in the rain of a thunderstorm. Danger surrounds you. You are like someone hunting a wild deer in the forest, where the path is overgrown and covered with brambles.

Look for a suitable guide; do not rush blindly toward your goal without help. You can only break through and achieve success in the proper way if you are patient.

ROOT

Advance slowly and carefully.
Learn with earnestness and sincerity.

Spring water flows down the mountain, and seminal truths are imparted. You are like a teacher initiating children in their first lesson. Although you scold those who do not pay attention, don't be hasty with punishment.

Attain your goal without using force. Be tolerant and generous, and success will come while you strive to improve yourself. If you try to reach for what is beyond your grasp, it will slip out of your hands.

NEEDS

Call upon the means by which we exist.

Water is still in the heavens, and has not yet fallen to the earth. The time is not yet ripe, and you should pause before taking action. Wait, and consider. Do not let yourself be influenced by selfish desires, and do not rely on luck alone to gain a victory.

Have faith in others, and trust in yourself. The right moment will come, and you will get through the situation by sailing effortlessly with the wind down the great water.

6

CONFLICT

Allow your disturbed opinions to be calmed,
and let mediation lead to peace.

Those in higher positions overwhelm those below them, and this leads to dispute. Winning a quarrel is nothing to be proud of, just as losing one is nothing to be ashamed of. A timely retreat leading to a harmonious solution is the best course of action.

Just like a war, the situation requires you to act fast and end the fight swiftly, so that there is no time for side issues or new problems to arise.

MULTITUDE

*Use the right strategies to take control of the
situation, just like directing an army.*

Water collects in the earth, and symbolizes the power of
many. You are the master of many soldiers, and you
subject them to the correct discipline. A motley rabble
cannot become an army, and no general can command a
disordered band.

Trust one with a noble character. Give authority and
power to able men instead of giving it to relatives or
those you know. Punish only the guilty, and do not
wrong an innocent person. Praise those who have
achieved something.

8

COMPLEMENT

Supplement your faith before you act.

Water is on the earth, and this is a good sign. Those below are subordinate to those above, and both have faith in each other. The most important thing to keep the situation from falling apart is for both parties to complement one another with the same faith.

At home, one depends on family.

In society, one depends on friends.

Follow this old saying, and build up a good social relationship with friends.

9

ACCUMULATING

Distance yourself from your old path.

The wind blows in the sky, gathering clouds, and rain is threatening but not yet falling. The time is not ripe for advancing, and difficulties still lie before you. It would be wise to spend time accumulating your power in readiness for when the right moment comes.

When circumstances are adverse, cherish the same ideals as before, and follow the same path as your friends and family. This way, you can be sure that the wheels will not separate from the axle.

RULES

Adhere strictly to correct rules.

Water is in the lower position, and heaven in the higher position, showing that things are proceeding according to the right rules. Subordinates respect their seniors in order to maintain harmony. It is better to stand on the earth than to attempt to walk on water.

Wear simple clothes, eat plain food, and think modestly. Fanciful thoughts will only lead to a false goal – just like treading on the tail of a tiger. Courage and daring alone cannot solve problems. It is important to recognize your own limits, and to gauge the actual strength of the opposing party. Handle matters in a decisive manner, but do not act rashly and carelessly.

PEACE

Come together with others without envy,
just as heaven blends with the earth.

The influence of heaven is below, and the energy of the earth is above. The high and the low mingle with each other, and majesty and humility share a mutual respect. This means good weather for crops, and clean air in politics. The country is prosperous, and the people live in peace.

The surface of the earth rises and falls – just like the ups and downs of life. To avoid misfortune, therefore, always remain aware and alert, even though currently peace and harmony prevail.

CENSURE

Retreat to cultivate your moral character.

Heaven remains above; earth remains below. The two energies are separated, and all creatures cannot be nourished and nurtured. Organizations exist in a state of discord, and those in high and low positions do not interact. This is how you risk losing the faith and trust of others.

Obeying the law of nature is the only way to change the situation. Be tolerant toward others, and do not waste a moment's thought on personal gains or losses. Only then will you be able to gather power, and finally sail through smooth waters.

COMMUNITY

Behave with faith and honesty,
leading to unity with others.

Fire is rising toward heaven, adding lustre to the dark night. The sun graces the sky with its light, radiating brightness everywhere. This indicates that high and low positions are coming together, and it is time for your great undertaking.

As long as you recognize that you are united with others, it will be advantageous to advance, and beneficial to hold your course.

POSSESSIONS

Prevent too much luxuriant growth.

It is a time of peace. The sun is shining in the sky, and there is fire in heaven. This warmth benefits myriad creatures, and brings forth a bumper harvest. But a bean that swells up too much will be torn apart, so it is important to prepare against danger before it is too late.

Strengthen your will to fight, and cultivate your work as you would cultivate a field. Conceal your success, and entrust your possessions to those with noble character. They will be able to help others benefit from your wealth, and this will guarantee your success.

15

MODESTY

Exercise humility and respect others,
and you will be respected in return.

The mountains stay below the earth, indicating that a person of noble character should remain humble. It is only because of your modesty that those who are immoral or corrupt defer to you.

The situation is like crossing a river: you can reach the other side safely only if you proceed with prudence and caution. This is the only way to maintain esteem, and to go forth into battle.

ENTHUSIASM

Realizing your error and repenting
in time can avert disaster.

The earth is awakened by thunder, and the myriad creatures are filled with vitality. It is time for you to act like a leader to make things happen. People will respond and support you.

Even if things are going smoothly, you should continue to strengthen your will, and abstain from wallowing in pleasure. Only in this way can you prevent bad influences from prevailing.

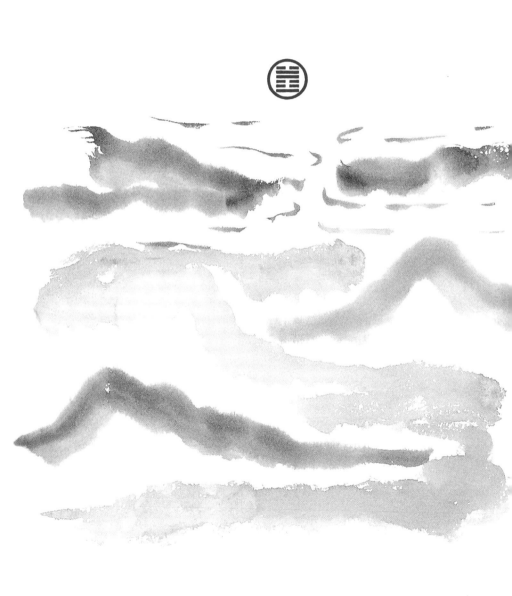

FOLLOWING

Ask, and also learn from, your subordinates.

This hexagram shows thunder below the sea – male power below female, and the higher position below the lower. Act as a noble person of moral integrity, and share your pleasure with others.

Consider yourself the equal of others, and thereby make everyone happy. This is the secret of maintaining your long-term happiness. If you do not seek personal gain, you will always gain.

DECAY

Remedy the situation courageously.

This hexagram tells of an insect springing up from old crops. It means the leader is reluctant to act, preferring instead a life of recreation. His people do the same – again, taking no action. Everyone is stuck in the same rut, dispirited and idle. Some may even start a rumor to create trouble, like a strong wind that blows toward the mountain: it will press down the grass, and snap off the branches of the trees.

With prosperity comes decay. It is important to issue orders now, and to repeat them again and again. Try to remedy the situation before killing the insect.

19

SUPERVISION

Govern people with gentleness
to earn their acquiescence.

After a period of complacency, it is necessary for you to supervise matters. This hexagram shows how the earth overlooks the water, embodying and forgiving all.

Control others to avoid error, but have faith in them. Supervise others with the wisdom appropriate to your status. Appear before others simply, and luck will come to you.

OBSERVATION

Show what you wish to be bestowed to others.

The wind moves over the earth without revealing itself. It is all-reaching, and influences the myriad creatures. It can observe everyone, and be observed by everyone. The wind is like you – it stays above the people, guarding them, and also giving orders, yet the people can also look upon it, and follow its example.

Educate others without using words. Set a good example, and people will behave in the proper way, without the need for further instruction.

BITING THROUGH

Enforce the law, and apply it the right way.

This is one of only two hexagrams in the entire I Ching that speaks directly of penalty. The hexagram shows thunder, shaking evil from below, while fire examines both the good and the bad from above. To bite cleanly you must remove sand, stones and bones before you can chew and swallow the food.

It is important to use both kindness and intimidation. Be sharp-sighted when using punishment; make sure you do not wrong an innocent person or let the guilty go free.

ADORNMENT

Adorn yourself beautifully at all times,
but follow the correct way closely.

It may seem that this hexagram speaks of outward appearance only, but never forget that the source of outer beauty is inner content. And beauty can only be admired through the right etiquette. Demonstrate your simplicity and frugality, and make your status respectable. You should only adorn yourself if you have the right inner substance.

Remain pure and modest, even though you might seem frugal sometimes. This will bring you success.

LAYING BARE

Take refuge at this time.

The legs of the bed are splitting apart, and it is dangerous for you to lie upon it. The situation is evident in the image of this hexagram: female power has overtaken male power. The base has turned upside down, and the roots are laid bare.

You must race against time to save the current state of affairs. Begin at the root of the problem, and stick to the truth. Then you will grow again.

RESUMPTION

Sow the right seeds.
Spring (thunder) awakens life once again.

Winter has left, and spring is returning. Life is resuming. If you have missed the path, you will meet one danger after another. Nonetheless, you will find the right direction sooner or later – if you follow good advice.

Continue on your way, acting correctly and righteously. Show no consideration for common customs, avoiding jealousy, gossip and slander, and disregard the suspicions of others. Honesty and sincerity will help you to carry on with your life.

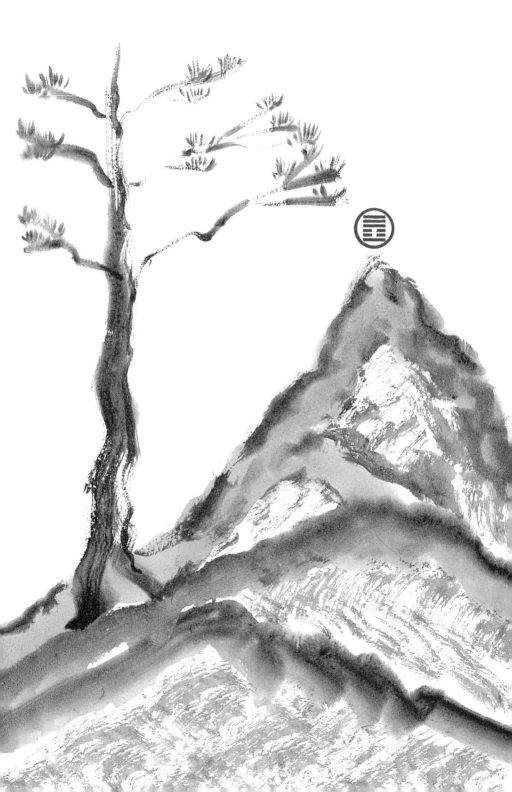

HONESTY

Let the seeds develop in their own way.

Thunder appears in the sky and awakens the myriad creatures, filling them with vitality. It is the right time to cultivate crops, but you must take care not to forge ahead; nothing can be forced to grow in a hurry.

A setback may occur, but if you adhere to the proper principles this event will resolve itself, and you will have an abundant harvest.

CULTIVATION

Model yourself on the words
and deeds of the sages.

Mountains embrace heaven, and this is the symbol of great cultivation. The mountain is quiet and generous, and that is why it can clutch the sky to its bosom.

Stop when you encounter a dangerous situation. Use the time to gather your power, restore your balance and hone your skills: this will aid your advancement. Do not fight against others, and do not show your real strength. Then you will find a smooth path ahead of you.

NOURISHMENT

Learn the deeper meaning of nourishment: taking food, but also cultivating moral character.

The thunder under the mountain gives warning. The leader should try to cultivate others, not the other way round. If you only eat and drink, without cultivating your moral character, you will meet danger.

Instead of watching others take their meals, it is better to look for your own food. Do not extort food from others, or you will risk losing their support. It is only when you can offer nourishment to others that success will come to you.

EXCESS

Find the balance between harshness and
gentleness, hardness and softness.

The branches of the tree weigh down heavily, as it has been irrigated with too much water. The pillar of an organization is close to breaking. Whatever grows too big cannot be governed, and whatever grows too vigorously may collapse. Model yourself on the wise person who knows how to find the right measure to deal with each subject.

Look for the proper way to rectify your mistakes. Salvage victory from defeat instead of waiting for disaster.

29

PITFALL

View the future carefully.
There are traps everywhere.

Water is above, and also below. There are dangers all around, and it is as though you are swimming in a torrent. You will make your way through only if you know the depth of the currents and the characteristics of the river.

Remain unhurried and calm, even if you face risk. Plant your feet on solid ground to keep yourself from sinking further into the situation. Then, step by step, you can move beyond the rapids.

BEAUTY

Move carefully, with respect.

An old day ends, and a new day begins. The sun rises to illuminate the earth. Beauty, warmth, brightness, distinction and clarity abound.

Act in an appropriate and deliberate manner, and proceed cautiously. Attach yourself to someone who is more competent than you, and your own ability will come into full play.

FEELING

Let male and female powers
combine with each other.

Here, the soft, female power of water is in a higher position, and the hard, male power of the mountain is in a lower position. This is the secret of how feeling can be reciprocated and transferred, and joy and harmony can be found. Unite your opinion with those of others.

You should not fight for a response, but remain steadfast in your position. It is better to look for unity of mind than to rush forward headlong.

CONSTANCY

Follow the law of nature, because
everything is bound by it.

Thunder is male, and holds the upper position; wind is female, and has the lower position. Let things function as they do in a traditional family. The husband directs the external world, and the wife hosts the internal world. Elder and younger, male and female, should follow the right order. The one in the upper position should speak and act cautiously, and be discreet and true in word and deed. The one in the lower position should behave gently and modestly. This is how a family should be regulated.

It is more important to maintain your proper position than to keep on moving. This is the only way to survive in the long run.

WITHDRAWAL

Withdraw in order to retain your dignity.

Heaven is too high to reach, and the mountain is too far away to protect you. Evildoers are closing in around you. It is dangerous to let yourself become engaged with old problems while living in seclusion.

Act like a noble person: withdraw while you are at the peak. Great fortune will descend upon you if you retire among the tributes.

GREAT STRENGTH

Gather power with the help of teachings, tactics,
willpower and determination.

Your strength has grown, but it is not yet time to go to battle. Learn when to advance, and when to retreat. Those who gain a victory through force will soon lose it again, just as the echo of thunder in the sky quickly fades.

A person of bad character conquers others using force; follow instead the example of those of noble character. Noble people win over the able, and enlist them to their cause.

35

ADVANCE

Develop your moral integrity and generosity.

The sun rises from the earth, bathing all the creatures in light. Though you might lose the trust of some people, face this with honesty, and detach yourself from suffering. Promotion and advancement in such a way will surely bring sorrow, therefore you need to earn the support of the multitude.

Promote those with the right abilities. Advance without being swayed by considerations of gain and loss. This approach will smooth the way before you.

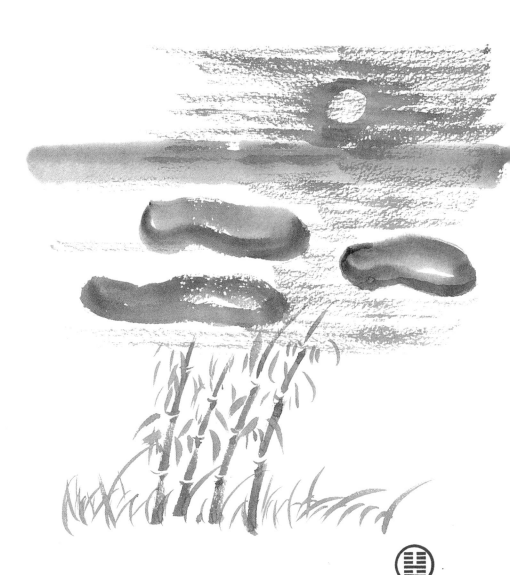

36

OBSCURITY

Clear a new space if the place surrounding
you is not favorable.

The sun has sunk below the horizon, and its brightness is lost. It is a difficult time; you had better keep a low profile, and stick to your principles. Do not put your trust in people lightly, but also do not lose your faith.

Work hard to move through complications, and adopt effective measures to turn bad luck into good.

FAMILY

Guard your moral character well, and protect
the harmony of your family.

In a traditional family, it is right for a woman to take care of the household duties, and also right for the man to look after matters outside the home. Be dignified in front of your children, and let each family member carry out their duties. Only in this manner can the family live in harmony. This is the basis of a successful nation and a peaceful world.

Prevention is better than a cure. Maintain honesty, and dignity will bring you luck.

SEPARATION

Avoid uncoordinated actions originating
from different wills.

The fire blazes upward, and the water surges downward. This points to a divergence of views, and suspicion of intentions. It does not help to worry about things that have been lost, or to fear evildoers.

Try to reconcile different opinions, and lead them toward the same goal. Gather the power of your family members together, and face each other with trust. Then you will welcome timely rainfall after a long drought.

OBSTRUCTION

*Depart courageously, for you will
return with honor.*

When you come across a gorge, it is wise to halt, and not advance. There is advantage in the southwest, and disadvantage in the northeast; try to use dignity to discover the correct way.

Do not automatically take the easy way. If you go against the current, you will attract the help of others. You will then meet with noble people, and improve your position.

RELEASE

Advance with the laws of nature, and combine
male and female power in harmony.

The thunderstorm releases obstructions, and it is favorable to move toward the southwest. Take quick action to resolve the situation, and this will bring luck.

After you have crossed the difficult water, advance with courage to create a new world. Cut yourself off from evil-doers to avoid interruptions and transgressions. Only then will those of noble character communicate with you, and will you move forward to fulfil a higher goal.

DECREASE

*Dispense with bad habits, and you
will gain unexpected profit.*

Mountains should be high, and the sea should be deep. Learn what should be decreased, and what should be increased, as demanded by the situation. With genuine sincerity, even very simple food can be offered to the gods as a sacrifice. The greatest achievement is to know how to balance decrease with increase – how to balance reduction and gain.

Restrain your anger, suppress your longings, and take no action without careful thought. It is better to move alone to avoid the suspicion and jealousy of others.

INCREASE

Correct your mistakes as fast as a thunderbolt,
and others will benefit.

Take from those in the upper position to benefit and satisfy those in the lower position. Then the wind will broadcast your good name, and you will sail with a favorable breeze. Never refuse an unexpected benefit, but remember its source, and express gratitude for it.

Once you are successful, do not rest on your laurels but continue to improve your situation for the benefit of others, just as you yourself have benefited. Your success may attract unwelcome attention, but remain kind-hearted. Have faith and courage, and you will be free from danger.

BREAKTHROUGH

Solve the problem without a fight
to save yourself from danger.

Water is in heaven, and will bring great change to the present situation. Do not proceed impetuously just because the goal is within your grasp. Do not start to fight while you can gain simply by advancing.

Stay alert, and take precautions against the enemy. Endure humiliation and a cold reception for the sake of the greater plan. Maintain the unity of your troops instead of crying bitterly. This will help you to move forward.

ENCOUNTER

*Hold back, and abstain at the first
encounter to protect yourself.*

This hexagram shows female power oppressing male power. It is like a woman chasing after a man, with only a thin sheet of paper to separate and protect him.

Act cautiously, and think deeply. Do not follow blindly, unless you wish to create the root of trouble for yourself.

ACCUMULATION

Use sincerity to endure the gathering.

The water gathers on the earth. Grass and trees flourish, symbolizing that the higher level pools its power with that of the lower level. You should take the chance to expand your domain.

After gathering the multitudes, convince everyone to advance together instead of worrying about difficulties. Hold fast to your own virtue, and let everyone find the right place. You will soon gain a new kingdom.

46

ASCENDANCE

*Follow the tree's example: grow slowly, and gather good
deeds from below, so that they rise up to perfection.*

Your modest and unassuming character is rising as a
result of the current situation. It is the right moment to
present yourself before the great person, and journey
toward the south.

Follow the situation, without pushing for results.
Announce your decision and your wish, and ask for
the support of others. Work together with them, with
one heart. Then you will rise to the top like an army
marching into an open city.

DISTRESS

Realize your error in time, and be repentant.
Then you can change your fortune.

The pond has a leak, and water cannot be retained. A dried-up pond symbolizes a lack of wealth. A noble person worries about lack of moral character, rather than a lack of possessions. Destitution is the best training for higher success, even if the period of distress lasts for a long time. When you face an arduous situation, try to hold onto a feeling of joy. This can help to smooth your future.

Rest, and build your strength. Abide by the law. Do not act before the foundations are solid. Learn the lesson of defeat so that you can advance with ease.

48

THE WELL

Bring the system into full play.

A well will benefit people only if its water is clean and it is fully functional. When old systems and laws are not used any more, they are inevitably abandoned. Execute the right law and the right system, like bringing a well into full use, and they will function automatically.

Carry out orders and implement systems rigorously so that others can work in peace and contentment. Only this way will it be advantageous for you.

49

TRANSFORMATION

*Earn the people's trust during the
process of transformation.*

Burning fire will dry out water; gushing water will extinguish fire. This is the process of transformation. Alterations are only possible in accordance with the laws of nature, and the common aspirations of people.

Apply the new laws only when the time is ripe. When the time comes, handle things in a decisive manner. Look after inner unity, instead of rushing into outward action. Earn the trust of the multitude, for their support can lead you to success.

50

THE CAULDRON

Light firewood for the great undertaking.

A traditional three-legged cooking pot is a country's heirloom, offering nourishment to all, and so leading to great progress as a nation. It symbolizes the highest power, and also the time for implementing a great plan. Collect materials for cooking before you light the fire. Then take care not to burn the food, or overturn the cooking pot.

Retreat to enjoy family life when you are losing power. Use your time to study the current situation carefully, and to solidify your development. Success will only come if you are law-abiding, and offer your cooperation to intelligent and capable subordinates.

AROUSAL

Reduce pressure. The more pressure there is,
the more resistance there will be.

The authority of a leader should rouse people like thunder. This is the only way laws and systems can be put into effect. People should be aroused first, and then they can enjoy peace.

Retain your dignity even when facing a battle. Make sure your standing has earned the respect of others; otherwise, you will not have the power to shake up the people and awaken them.

HALT

Stop while there's time to stop, and act
while there's time to act.

Too much talk leads to failure. The more you promise, the less people will trust you. You can only lead people with honesty and kindheartedness.

Get the timing right, and it will lead you to enlightenment. Find the correct balance between motion and inactivity, restraint and interference, and this will improve your situation. To know your own limits, and to retreat if necessary, will ensure you are protected from misfortune.

53

PROGRESS

Hold the right course, and advance gradually.

Pursue the right path, just like the flight of the wild goose. The goose begins near the shore and advances to the rocks, then goes on to farmlands and trees, up to the hills, and finally reaching the high mountains and the sky.

Do not rest at the wrong place; continue your journey to avoid danger. Do not do things out of sequence, for only by following in the correct footsteps can you experience success.

WEDDING MAIDEN

Treat each event as the marriage of a daughter.

The wedding of a maiden is the most important event in the world. It is just like a union of heaven and earth, without which life cannot continue.

Behave like a young married woman who traditionally obeys her husband, upholds morality, speaks impeccably, is modest, and works diligently to fulfil her duties. If you act like this, you will soon be blessed with abundance.

ABUNDANCE

Retain modesty and you will
retain abundance.

It is midday, and the sun is at its highest point. Soon it will begin to set, and dusk will close in, clouding its brightness.

Retain your bright character, and follow the right leader. Only then will you continue to grow.

56

JOURNEY

Remain detached, and deal with
the matter resolutely.

A fire cannot burn all the time, just as a traveler cannot continue without rest, and an event cannot develop without end. You may gain something, or you may lose something. Either way, you are travelling in an unknown land, and so you must advance carefully. Uphold your principles, and observe things sharply – like a fire above – while handling your affairs as steadily as the mountain that rests below.

The only way to get along in a strange place is to occupy a suitable position. Never forget that even a dragon cannot defeat a snake in the snake's own territory.

57

OBEDIENCE

Behave with the courage of a warrior,
and uphold your principles.

Wind carries wind, and influence moves influence. It is favorable to advance, and it is advantageous to meet the great person. You must wait patiently for things to develop. Adhere to the heart of the matter, use the correct method, make decisions with resolve, battle vigorously, and live in moderation. This will lead others to submit to you, and help you to reach your goal.

Upholding justice will lessen your risk. If you obey because you are forced, or if you make others obey you through force, you will never find the right path.

58

HAPPINESS

*Lead people with gentleness and kindness, but maintain
your own fortitude and resourcefulness.*

Appear gentle, but uphold your principles firmly within
yourself. Persist in your opinion, but do not be obstinate.
Treat people in a friendly manner, without flattering
them. You will enjoy the resulting pleasure of swimming
in refreshingly cool and clear water.

Stay away from gossipmongers. Their talk may be jovial,
but in the end they will only distract you from your path.
Distance yourself from people of bad character, and this
will help you to avoid trouble.

DISPERSION

Bow down before an official or leader,
and you will spread your sails.

The wind blows over the water, and disperses the power that has gathered. Wait for a quiet moment in which to make your move. In the meantime, work strenuously – combining others' efforts – to remedy the slack situation. Your benevolent leadership will encourage others to fuel your brilliance.

Hold the correct position, and use an appropriate motto to enlist the cooperation of the multitude. Lead people with faith and honesty, and you will not lose their steady, combined power.

MODERATION

Learn the correct measure of
distribution and collection.

Still waters turn into a swamp, and a rolling stone gathers no moss. It is important, therefore, to find the right balance between release and accumulation.

Be moderate in your actions, and do not waste resources. Undue moderation, however, is not effective, and this is why it is important to find the correct balance between discipline and moderation for the current situation.

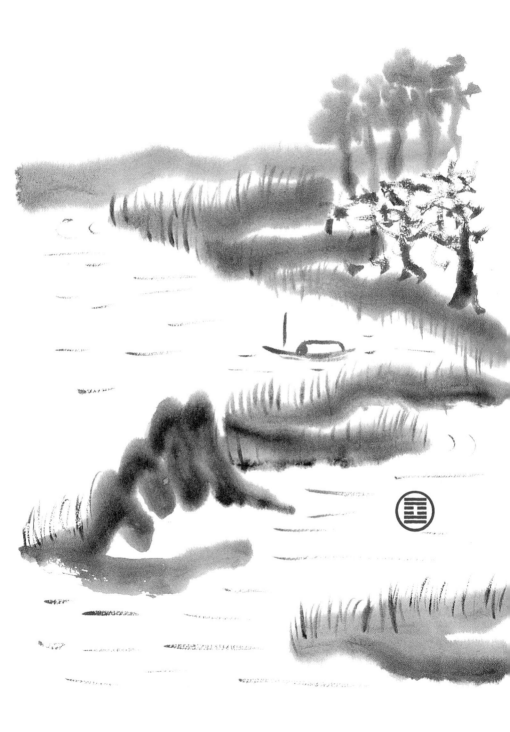

INNER TRUTH

Move forward with honesty;
unite your thoughts and actions.

This hexagram shows the wind blowing over the surface of the water, and making a clearing in the middle. It means that you should empty and open your mind in order to learn from others, and behave with modesty toward yourself.

Pass judgement with faith, and handle matters with loyalty. This attitude will help you to win the hearts of everyone.

MINOR ACHIEVEMENT

Remain lower rather than higher, and act
smaller rather than greater.

The power of thunder is decreased by the mountain. You are acting bigger than you are, and this will lead to futility. It is time to accept a modest assignment, and this modesty will bring you luck.

Taking precautions against unexpected attack is better than rushing to overstep the mark. Flaunting your superiority will only bring you trouble.

ACCOMPLISHMENT

Maintain what you have achieved.
This is even harder than starting something new.

The female power of water combines with the male power of fire. When this comes into full effect, they can either achieve great success or damage each other, leading to disaster. There is danger hidden within good fortune, and turmoil within peace.

Being vigilant during times of peace is the best way to avoid danger. Always remember that the beginning follows the end, and the end follows the beginning.

64

STRIVING TO ACCOMPLISH

Continue to improve yourself, and continue to benefit others.

Male and female powers beget each other. Life and death follow each other. The new and the old replace each other. Top and bottom complement each other. Success and failure supplement each other. This is the circle of nature and the I Ching.

Follow the example of heaven and earth to continue progressing. The accomplishments you have achieved are not just the end of a paragraph: they are also the beginning of a new chapter. You have not yet reached the peak of your success, and are already facing a new challenge. Just as heaven and earth keep moving to nurture the myriad creatures, you should continue to accomplish your duties. That is the only way to reach the summit.

ABOUT THE AUTHOR

CHAO-HSIU CHEN is a renowned artist, philosopher and musician who was born in Taiwan, where she grew up with the influences of Taoism, Confucianism and Buddhism – the foundation of her wide knowledge and deep understanding of Chinese philosophies and wisdom. She went on to study music in Vienna and Salzburg, composing music for television. Chao is the author of over forty books, which have been translated into more than twenty languages, and her paintings are regularly exhibited around the world.

Visit Chao's website at:
www.chaohsiuchen.com

EDDISON BOOKS LIMITED

MANAGING DIRECTOR Lisa Dyer
CREATIVE CONSULTANT Nick Eddison
MANAGING EDITOR Tessa Monina
DESIGNER Brazzle Atkins
PRODUCTION Sarah Rooney & Cara Clapham